THE GOLDEN YEAR

1972

text: David Sandison, Micheal Heatley, Lorna Milne, Ian Welch

design: Yael Hodder

SIENA

197

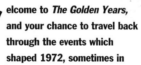

Welcome to *The Golden Years,* and your chance to travel back through the events which shaped 1972, sometimes in dramatic fashion, but often in ways we'd only see as important when the passing of time cleared the dust away. It would, for example, be some time before the world would know the full truth which lay behind the arrest in June of five men caught breaking into the Watergate building offices occupied by the Democratic Party's election headquarters.

For the time being, in 1972, Richard Nixon played a remarkable carrot-and-stick game with the communist super-powers. US troops may have left South Vietnam, but B-52s were capable of bombing Hanoi to the conference table.

Talking appeared, sadly, to have stopped in Ulster, where the tragic events of Londonderry's 'Bloody Sunday' in January would continue to resound around the province for many years to come. Prime Minister Edward Heath began to face domestic troubles with trade unions which would end with Britain's wages, rents and prices frozen In a bid to retain some control.

In Uganda, dictator Idi Amin proved he'd lost control - of reality - when he began deporting hundreds of thousands of Asians he accused of sabotaging the economy his regime had already destroyed.

Noted departures from the world stage included the Duke of Windsor and FBI chief J Edgar Hoover. The arrival on the London stage of *Jesus Christ Superstar,* a new musical by newcomers Tim Rice and Andrew Lloyd Webber, raised a controversial storm.

There was no doubt about world opinion of the tragic events which overtook the Olympic Games in Munich. What was meant to be a celebration of the heights to which gifted young athletes could soar, it became a terrible glimpse of just how low people could sink as Palestinian terrorists murdered young Israelis.

But it wasn't all so grim, as you'll discover and recall. There were silver linings in those clouds. 1972 was, after all, one of *The Golden Years.*

A Queen Goes Up In Smoke

THE FORMER CUNARD ocean liner *Queen Elizabeth* was severely damaged by fire today as she lay moored in Hong Kong Harbour. Fire-fighting tugs struggled in vain to save the vessel which was launched in the 1930s and served until 1969 as a holiday cruise ship in peacetime and a troopship during the war.

For the last few years *Queen Elizabeth* had been home to students of the Seawise University in Hong Kong. Initial investigations suggested that the fire may have been started deliberately.

The liner's burned-out hulk would eventually be sold to a US company, taken to California and refitted as a permanent conference and events centre.

JANUARY 12

Bangladesh Has New Premier

Sheikh Mujibur Rahman became the first Prime Minister of the new independent nation of Bangladesh today, just four days after he was released from nine months' imprisonment in Pakistan.

Rahman, leader of the Awami (People's) League, had long been under threat of death for his leadership of that Bengali liberation movement in the former East Pakistan, but was reprieved by Zulfikar Ali Bhutto when he came to power in West Pakistan.

The 52-year-old visionary now led a country with the densest population in the world, living on a land which was prone to extensive flooding. Britain's recognition of Bangladesh would lead to the withdrawal of Pakistan from the British Commonwealth later in the month.

JANUARY 1

Farewell To Charming Chevalier

Maurice Chevalier, the French entertainer beloved for his charm, which seemed to combine old-world refinement with a certain Gallic je *ne sais quoi*, died today at the age of 83,

He did not have an easy start to life, being the ninth child of an alcoholic house painter, and he was forced to abandon a successful teenage career as an acrobat when he became injured. Performing was in his blood, however, and he began to gain popularity in the French music-halls.

Chevalier spent much of the First World War as a prisoner of war, and was much criticized for his performances in Germany during the WWII. A film career that spanned the pre and post-war years included his best-known movie, the award-winning *Gigi* in 1958, in which he immortalized Lerner and Loewe's *Thank Heaven For Little Girls*.

JANUARY 30

Thirteen Slain On Ulster's Bloody Sunday

AN APPARENTLY PEACEFUL civil rights march in Londonderry turned into a massacre today when British paratroopers fired on the demonstrators, killing 13 and wounding another 17. Local politicians immediately dubbed the tragedy as 'Bloody Sunday' and attacked military handling of the march and its aftermath, although British Army chiefs maintained that the soldiers had begun firing in self-defence.

The violence erupted as Republican civil rights demonstrators tried to break down a roadblock in the city's Bogside area and the troops began to open fire, initially with rubber bullets and water-cannon spraying purple dye, but then with live rounds.

Over a hundred rioters hurled stones and other missiles at the soldiers, and eye-witness reports said that the first shot was, in fact, fired by a Loyalist gunman. In the ensuing battle it was impossible to say who had shot whom. The IRA earlier in the month had planted a bomb in a Belfast department store which injured 55 women and children, so tension was already high in the province.

JANUARY 31

Thousands Mourn Gospel Great Mahalia

The funeral of legendary American gospel singer Mahalia Jackson, who died four days ago, aged 60, attracted more than 40,000 mourners who filed past her open casket in Greater Salem Baptist Church in Chicago, today.

Born in New Orleans, Mahalia Jackson had established her superstar status despite never crossing over to secular music, the route taken by many of her peers. Soul star Aretha Franklin, one of many to be influenced by records made by Miss Jackson in a recording career that began in 1946, sang at her funeral the next day, while a message from President Nixon was read to a congregation that included Chicago's Mayor Richard Daley and entertainer Sammy Davis Jr.

JANUARY 22

Britain In Europe At Last

Britain was one of four countries to join the European Economic Community today when Prime Minister Edward Heath signed the Treaty of Brussels to end ten long years of negotiation Norway, Denmark and Ireland joined at the same time.

When Britain's membership took full effect in a year's time, the new EEC would comprise ten member states and boast a larger combined population than either the United States or Soviet Russia, and be responsible for more than 40 per cent of world trade.

Today's ceremony marked a personal victory for Mr Heath who, as Lord Privy Seal, became Britain's chief negotiator for EEC membership in the early 1960s, an attempt which failed because of French resistance. This time, his second time round, Mr Heath - who had always promoted European unity - convinced not only the 'Six' original EEC members, but also his Conservative Party and the UK electorate, that membership was vital for Britain.

JANUARY 19

British TV Bursts Forth

Britain's Minister of Posts and Telecommunications, former Olympic athlete Christopher Chataway, today announced that he would no longer exercise his powers under the Telecommunications Act to control the hours TV was allowed to broadcast.

The result of this decision was to create the greatest increase in the number of new shows to hit British screens since the launch of independent television as a rival to the BBC back in 1955. With daytime TV now available, programme makers had 20 more hours of viewing time to fill. They chose to use them for the introduction of a new generation of soap operas, quizzes, comedy and current affairs shows.

FEB

Palace Coup In Qatar

A bloodless palace coup in the tiny Gulf state of Qatar saw Shaikh Ahmad deposed by his cousin Shaikh Khalifa ibn Hamad al-Thani today.

Qatar had been under British influence since a treaty effectively handed control to Westminster in 1916. At the beginning of the 1970s, however, a plan was developed for future independent elections in the country after control was handed over to the al-Thanis, Qatar's principal ruling family.

Control still rested with the al-Thanis after today's coup, but democratic elections were still nowhere in sight.

Grease Is The Word

Grease, a musical in fashionably nostalgic vein, opened today in New York, in an off-Broadway theatre.

With its gentle parodies of 1950s music and morals, *Grease* would prove enough of a success after four months of packed houses to move into the much bigger and more prestigious Broadhurst Theatre on Broadway. There, it would run continuously until April 1980, eclipsing *Fiddler On The Roof* as Broadway's longest-running production.

Most famously, of course, *Grease* would be turned into a hit movie, starring John Travolta and Olivia Newton-John, six years later.

Dublin Rioters Destroy British Embassy

THE BRITISH EMBASSY in Dublin was destroyed today when demonstrators taking part in a march to mark the deaths of 13 people last month in Londonderry attacked the building with fire-bombs.

Today had been declared an official day of mourning by the Republic of Ireland Government, but what was to have been a solemn marking of the 'Bloody Sunday' deaths degenerated into scenes of angry anti-British violence when crowds attacked the Georgian building which housed the Embassy, reducing it to rubble.

Police officers at the scene were completely outnumbered by protesters and appeared powerless to intervene. In fact, it wasn't until after the Embassy roof had collapsed that fire-fighters were allowed into the area to try - and fail - to extinguish the blaze.

The Blackout Is Back

Large areas of Britain were plunged into darkness today as nine-hour electricity cuts caused the most extensive blackouts since the end of World War II. With the country in the grip of a long coalminers' strike and a total of 12 coal-fired power stations already shut down to conserve diminishing fuel reserves, all industry was on a three-day working week and Britons had been asked to heat just one room of their homes to save electricity.

Faced with this new crisis, the UK Government declared a state of emergency. That emergency deepened a week later when ASLEF, the train-drivers' union, announced that it was ordering its members not to cross miners' picket lines, thus impeding the transport of vital coal and oil supplies to remaining power stations.

A settlement would not be finally reached until early March.

UK TOP 10 SINGLES

1: Telegram Sam
- T Rex

2: Son Of My Father
- Chicory Tip

3: Mother Of Mine
- Neil Reid

4: Have You Seen Her
- The Chi-Lites

5: I'd Like To Teach The World To Sing
- The New Seekers

6: Horse With No Name
- America

7: Look Wot You Dun
- Slade

8: Let's Stay Together
- Al Green

9: American Pie
- Don McLean

10: Brand New Key
- Melanie

Born this month:
9: Darren Ferguson, Scotland Under-21 international football player
11: Steve McManaman, English international football player

DEPARTURES

Died this month:
5: Marianne Moore, American poet, aged 84
15: Edgar Snow, American writer, aged 66
28: Viktor Barna, Hungarian table tennis ace - world champion 1930, 1932-5

FEBRUARY 24

West Germany Pays Ransom

The hijacking of a West German Lufthansa 747 paid off handsomely for the Arab terrorists who carried out the raid, when the West German Government caved in to demands for a $5 million ransom today. The hijackers had boarded the jumbo jet at Aden, forcing it to fly to the Indian capital, New Delhi.

While the families of the hostages were naturally grateful for the safe return of their loved ones, the acquiescence of a major Western power to the demands of the terrorists seemed certain to encourage similar incidents in the future. In the US, tougher security measures were introduced at airports.

FEBRUARY 17

Moon Rises Over The Rainbow

The rock world received its first taste of a monumental piece of music - Pink Floyd's *Dark Side Of The Moon* - tonight in London when the suite was unveiled at the start of a four-night residency at the Rainbow Theatre.

A work which, when released as a concept album in 1973, would top charts worldwide and go on to sell in excess of 20 million copies, *Dark Side Of The Moon* was an unlikely candidate for such success, given that its subject matter was the descent into mental illness.

The undeniable grandeur of the music was acclaimed by a capacity crowd tonight. Three of the four members of Pink Floyd who presented the work tonight - David Gilmour, Rick Wright and Nick Mason - would still be on board in 1994 when the suite was re-recorded live for inclusion in the group's best-selling *PULSE* in-concert double album.

FEBRUARY 22

Aldershot Rocked By Car Bomb

The IRA's chosen revenge for last month's 'Bloody Sunday' killings in Northern Ireland left seven dead when a 50-pound car bomb exploded today outside the barracks of the 16th Parachute Brigade in Aldershot, Hampshire. The soldiers involved in the Londonderry massacre were predominantly paratroopers.

Not a single soldier was injured in today's blast, but five of the dead were women who were preparing lunch in the kitchens of the officers' mess. The other victims were a gardener and a Catholic padre, Captain Gerry Weston.

The attack, for which no warning was given, prompted the British Army to instigate a complete review of security on all its bases and properties, which meant the end of so-called 'open' barracks such as those in Aldershot, historically regarded as the home of the British Army.

Pragmatic Nixon Woos Chinese

PRESIDENT RICHARD NIXON'S week-long visit to mainland China, which ended today, was hailed as a major breakthrough in Sino-American relations, despite the fact that there were no plans announced for the two countries to resume formal diplomatic relations. Both nations appeared keen to thaw what had long been a decidedly cool relationship, but the major stumbling block was the US' continued recognition of Chiang Kai-shek's Nationalist regime in Taiwan.

Although President Nixon declared that the ultimate aim of the US was to withdraw American military personnel from Taiwan, observers suggested that this was unlikely to happen in the immediate future.

Nevertheless, Nixon - a long-time and vociferous opponent of Communism - believed that his meetings with Chairman Mao Tse-tung and premier Chou En-lai would help to bring about a 'generation of peace'. Even his fiercest critics had to admit that the President's visit was a statesman-like gesture from a man who was, above all, a realist and pragmatist.

FEB

MAR

Heath Introduces Direct Rule For Ulster

THE LATEST AND MOST HORRIFIC in a series of violent attacks by the IRA – the death on March 21 of six people and the injuring of 146 others in a Belfast department store after a hoax caller deliberately misled police over the location of a bomb – resulted in today's announcement by British Prime Minister Edward Heath that the Northern Irish parliament at Stormont was to be suspended, and that Ulster was to be ruled direct from Westminster.

The news was greeted with dismay by Ulster Unionists, who accused the government of caving in to IRA violence. However, there was wide support from both sides of the House of Commons, and from the Irish Republic's Government in Dublin.

Explaining his decision in a networked TV broadcast, Mr Heath told the Irish people: 'Now is your chance. A chance for fairness, a chance for prosperity, and a chance for peace- a chance at last to bring the bombings and killings to an end'.

Manley Follows In Father's Footsteps

Michael Manley, son of Jamaica's first Prime Minister, Norman Washington Manley, led the People's National Party to victory in elections today. Appointed to the Senate by his father in the early 1960s, Michael Manley was subsequently elected to the House of Representatives and, on his father's retirement in 1969, had taken over as leader of the party his father had founded.

His win, following a campaign based on wide-ranging social reforms, marked the beginning of what would be only his first term in office as premier.

Gary Glitters – By Gadd!

Britain gained a new, and unlikely, pop hero today with the release of the first single by Gary Glitter, a pseudonym concealing pop music veteran Paul Gadd whose previous aliases included Paul Raven, Paul Monday and Gutbucket.

The record's B-side, *Rock & Roll Part 2*, consisted of little more than a thudding drumbeat and a succession of animal grunts, but it was this which would prove the hit, setting a successful pattern that would yield three UK chart-toppers and nine more Top 10 entries, of which this was one.

Glitter's secret was not taking the new glam-rock movement too seriously, performing it with a leer and a knowing wink. He would survive well into the 1990s, beating drink and drugs excesses (expounded upon in his entertaining autobiography) as well as Father Time to influence a whole new generation.

Although *Rock & Roll Part 2* only reached No 2, it would go one better in 1988 at the hands of The Timelords (Bill Drummond and Jimmy Cauty), who retitled it *Doctorin' The Tardis*.

Jupiter Probe Launched

The most ambitious space exploration plan ever was put into operation today when the US' space probe *Pioneer 10* was launched on a 21-month voyage to the planet Jupiter.

Although the probe, with four nuclear generators propelling it towards its goal, would get no closer than 100,000 miles to the giant planet, it was hoped that it could send photographs back to Earth of over two-thirds of Jupiter's surface.

Even then, its mission would not be over. The spacecraft was designed to head for outer space, with an Earth-style greeting for any extraterrestrials it might encounter.

UK TOP 10 SINGLES

1: Without You
- Nilsson
2: American Pie
- Don McLean
3: Son Of My Father
- Chicory Tip
4: Beg Steal Or Borrow
- The New Seekers
5: Mother And Child Reunion
- Paul Simon
6: Got To Be There
- Michael Jackson
7: Blue Is The Colour
- Chelsea FC
8: Alone Again (Naturally)
- Gilbert O'Sullivan
9: Look Wot You Dun
- Slade
10: Meet Me On The Corner
- Lindisfarne

East Berlin Opens Its Gates

BERLIN - THE GERMAN CITY which had sat uncomfortably astride the Iron Curtain since the end of World War II, when it was split in two, with the eastern half governed by a Soviet-dominated Communist regime, and the western section governed by the Allies - went some way towards reconciling East and West today when restrictions on West Berliners travelling to the eastern half of the city were relaxed for the first time in 20 years.

Later in the year, the first air links between East and West Germany were created in a welcome atmosphere of *détente*. This led, in November, to the signing of a treaty in the West German capital, Bonn, to normalize relations, though it wouldn't be until 1989 that the Berlin Wall - erected in the early 1960s - would finally come down.

MARCH 25

New Seekers Fail To Find Euro-Prize

Broadcast from the Usher Hall in Edinburgh and presented by Moira Shearer, the Eurovision Song Contest failed to produce a home win for Britain. The New Seekers' jaunty *Beg Steal Or Borrow* was beaten into second place by Vicky Leandros's thunderous ballad *Aprés Toi,* which took the honours for Luxembourg.

In UK chart terms, honours proved even when both reached No 2, with *Aprés Toi* retitled *Come What May.* Leandros, who was actually from Greece, only managed one more chart entry before returning to anonymity.

MARCH 13

Hughes Autobiography A Hoax

A New York court today heard a confession by author Clifford Irving that he had made up the 'autobiography' of reclusive millionaire Howard Hughes (pictured). In a swindle that scandalized New York's publishing community, Irving had convinced major publishers McGraw-Hill that he had gained hundreds of interviews with Hughes in order to write the book. After giving the fraudster a $750,000 advance, the publishers went into overdrive publicizing what they believed to be the scoop of the century. Sadly, Irving had misjudged Hughes, whom he wrongly believed to be either dead or mentally incapable. His fraud was exposed when Hughes called *Time* magazine, who were serializing the book, t o say he'd never met Irving!

Heath Acts To Save Boy In Turkish Jail

Aware of a mounting nationwide campaign for his release, British Prime Minister Edward Heath today pledged to do everything he could to help Timothy Davey, the 14-year-old London boy recently sentenced to six years in a Turkish prison for conspiring to sell cannabis.

Despite appeals for clemency by successive British governments, the youngster would not be released until May 1974, and then only as a result of a nationwide amnesty following the election of a new President. His ordeal would inspire Alan Parker's 1978 film, *Midnight Express*.

'GODFATHER' WINS BIG, BUT 'CABARET' STEALS MORE OSCARS

While this year has rightly gone down in movie history as the one in which *The Godfather* established a host of world box-office records and walked off with the Academy Award as Best Picture, for Marlon Brando's Best Actor win in the title role, and the Oscar shared by Mario Puzo and director Francis Ford Coppola for the screenplay they adapted from Puzo's best-selling novel, it's worth remembering that's all *The Godfather* did win, despite 11 major nominations.

The honours at this year's Oscars ceremony were in fact taken by the eight awards won by *Cabaret,* the directorial debut of choreographer Bob Fosse who translated the hit stage musical based on Christopher Isherwood's racy memoirs of pre-World War II Berlin into one of the greatest ever pieces of cinematic art.

So it was Fosse and not Coppola who won the Oscar as Best Director. It was Liza Minnelli who won the Best Actress award for her wondrous Sally Bowles. It was Joel Grey who was given the Supporting Actor Oscar as the sleazy MC, cameraman Geoffrey Unsworth who took the Cinematography prize, editor David Bretherton who was adjudged winner of his category, Ralph Burns whose arrangements won him the Adaptation or Original Song Score statuette, the wonderfully evocative period sets of Rolf Zehetbauer and Jurgen Kiebach which won the Art Direction Oscar and the team of Robert Knudsen and David Hilyard which walked off with the Best Sound prize.

The trail of brave losers left by Minnelli and Grey speaks volumes for their achievements. Minnelli saw off the challenges of Diana Ross (for her bio-pic of Billie Holiday, *Lady Sings The Blues*), Cicely Tyson (for *Sounder*), Maggie Smith (*Travels With My Aunt*) and Liv Ullman (for *The Emigrants*). And Grey was victorious in a final nominations list of James Caan, Robert Duvall and Al Pacino (all in *The Godfather*), and Eddie Albert (for *The Heartbreak Kid*).

Amid all this, a few of the year's most notable hits got lost as far as awards were concerned. Marlon Brando's win meant the end of either Michael Caine or Sir Laurence Olivier picking up Oscars for *Sleuth,* though they could share the disappointment with director Joseph L Mankiewicz, who lost out to Bob Fosse, along with John Boorman (for *Deliverance,* another hit which missed out) and Jan Troell (*The Emigrants*).

Jeremy Larner picked up the Original Screenplay Oscar for the otherwise overlooked Robert Redford thriller *The Candidate,* and while Shelley Winters was nominated for a Supporting Actress award for *The Poseidon Adventure,* she had to concede victory to Eileen Heckart for *Butterflies Are Free,* while the producers of the upside-down sea thriller

had to be content with millions of dollars at the box office, an Oscar for Al Kasha and Joel Hirchhorn's song *The Morning After,* and the Visual Effects prize collected by LB Abbott and AD Flowers.

Charlie Chaplin won a statuette to add to the Honorary Oscar the Academy had presented to him a year earlier in a moving welcome back to Hollywood after 30 years in exile - this time for his score for *Limelight.*

Footnote: a cynic once remarked that you could always tell when a veteran star was about to die - Hollywood would always rectify the lack of an Oscar won during a long career by presenting an Honorary Oscar. This year, Edward G Robinson was awarded such a tribute. He died soon after.

Liza Minnelli in the Oscar winning 'Cabaret'

APRIL

APRIL 11

Jenkins Jumps Over Europe

Roy Jenkins was the most senior of a group of Labour shadow ministers who quit the Opposition's front bench today over what they saw as the Labour Party's equivocation on a national referendum to decide whether or not Britain should join the European Economic Community.

Along with Harold Lever, George Thomson and David Owen, Jenkins had fallen out with Labour leader Harold Wilson's decision to support rebel Conservative anti-EEC campaigners' calls for a referendum. They believed it would result in a resounding 'No' to the Common Market entry terms negotiated by Edward Heath's government.

While Labour was largely anti-EEC, the objection of Jenkins and Co - mostly pro-EEC- was said to be mainly in protest over Wilson's unholy alliance with right-wing members of 'the enemy'.

APRIL 27

Oxford Colleges To Get Gentle Touch

Five of Oxford University's men-only colleges today announced they were to admit women students for the first time. The experiment, which was to run for five years, would commence in October 1974, leaving 19 other Oxford campuses considering whether or not to follow suit.
The first five colleges to drag themselves into the 20th century were Jesus, Wadham, Brasenose, St Catherine's and Hertford.

APRIL 1

Sea, Sun And Bloodshed In Puerto Rico

The three-day, 30,000-spectator Mar Y Sol (Sea and Sun) Festival, held in Puerto Rico, brought with it the blackest vibes since Altamont in 1969. Despite the presence of big rock names like Black Sabbath, The Allman Brothers, Emerson Lake and Palmer and The Mahavishnu Orchestra, the event would go down in history for no fewer than four fatalities. One was a 16-year-old boy, reportedly hacked to death in his sleeping-bag.

Hundreds of US fans were stranded at the airport after the festival, which the Puerto Rican Minister of Health had apparently tried in vain to ban, fearing what he described as 'a plague of drug abuse'. It seemed like everything else happened instead.

18

North Vietnam – Nixon Orders Increased Bombing

WITH SOUTH VIETNAM under severe and increased pressure from a massive Vietcong force which launched a powerful attack across the demilitarized zone earlier this month to occupy much of Quangtri province with little resistance, President Nixon today ordered US Air Force commanders to strike back at North Vietnam with concerted bombing raids on the capital, Hanoi, and its neighbouring port of Haiphong.

The first major raids for almost four years, their principal targets were warehouse and fuel supplies in the capital and areas of Haiphong where Russian-made and supplied arms and ammunition were known to be stored.

It was widely believed that the Communist government in Hanoi had launched the latest offensive to create domestic anti-war protests in the US, and was fearful that the Americans would negotiate an end to the Vietnamese war with the Soviet Union and China, both of whose regimes supported the Vietcong's struggle.

Ulster Crisis Lurches On

The British Government's decision to rule Ulster directly from Westminster did not appear to have changed things in the province this month, as events transpired.

On April 3, Belfast city centre was brought to a halt as thousands of Catholic women staged a demonstration in support of the IRA. Ten days later, their heroes and Loyalist opponents combined their 'skills' to detonate no fewer than 23 bombs in the worst day of violence since the introduction of direct rule. Fuel was added to the flames of dissent on April 19 when an official inquiry into the 'Bloody Sunday' shootings said that, while there was no doubt British troops had been provoked, some of the soldiers had fired recklessly into crowds of fleeing civil rights demonstrators.

UK TOP 10 SINGLES

1: Without You
- Nilsson
2: Beg Steal Or Borrow
- The New Seekers
3: Amazing Grace
- The Royal Scots Dragoon Guards
4: Sweet Talkin' Guy
- The Chiffons
5: Hold Your Head Up
- Argent
6: Back Off Boogaloo
- Ringo Starr
7: Alone Again (Naturally)
- Gilbert O'Sullivan
8: The Young New Mexican Puppeteer
- Tom Jones
9: Desiderata
- Les Crane
10: Heart Of Gold
- Neil Young

APRIL 22

British Couple Cross Pacific In Rowing-Boat

Islanders seen rowing Britannia II into Betio Harbour, Tarawa, Gilbert Islands after it struck a reef, Jan 19th.

JOHN FAIRFAX, the man who rowed single-handedly across the Atlantic in 1969, today completed another record by rowing across the vast Pacific Ocean with his girlfriend, Sylvia Cook, a former secretary from Surrey in their boat Britannia II.

The couple's epic trip, which ended triumphantly this evening on Hayman's Island, off Australia's Queensland coast, had taken just short of a year to complete – 361 days, to be precise, from the time they left San Francisco.

Nothing had been seen or heard of the pair since they passed the Solomon Islands eight weeks previously and there were fears that recent cyclones had overcome their tiny craft. But this was one voyage that, fortunately, was to have a happy ending.

APRIL 27

Moon Rocks Fall To Earth

More than 200 pounds of rocks from the Moon splashed into the Pacific today, aboard the returning capsule of *Apollo 16.* Astronauts John Young and Charles Duke had spent 11 days exploring the surface of the Moon, while Thomas Mattingly manned the command ship in its lunar orbit. The *Apollo 16 and 17* missions explored the Moon's highlands with the aid of a wheeled Lunar Rover, the so-called 'Moon Buggy', while the total weight of Moon rocks brought back to Earth for analysis by all the *Apollo* missions exceeded 900 pounds.

APRIL 29

Sometime In New York City

Ex-Beatle John Lennon today won support for his fight to stay in the United States from an unexpected source – New York City's mayor, John Lindsay. Having had his residence visa extension cancelled by the New York Office of the Department of Immigration the previous month - just five days after it had been issued - Lennon was pleased to hear Lindsay's plea to stop threatened deportation proceedings.

Referring to Lennon and his Japanese-born wife, Yoko Ono – the subject of similar proceedings who feared she might thereby lose custody of a daughter from a previous marriage – Mayor Lindsay said their plight was 'a grave injustice in light of their unique contributions in the fields of music and art'.

MAY 2

FBI Chief Hoover Checks Out

J Edgar Hoover, the man whose name was synonymous with America's FBI law enforcement agency for close on 50 years, died today at the age of 77.

Appointed director of the FBI in 1924 – although at that time it was just the Bureau of Investigation, the 'Federal' was added in 1935 – Hoover remained in the post for 48 years, serving under eight US Presidents. (*See Came & Went pages for full biography*)

MAY 5

Guitarist Gary Picks His Last

The blind blues guitarist, the Reverend Gary Davis, suffered a fatal heart attack in Hammonton, New Jersey, today. Aged 76, he was famed as a performer in the ragtime, blues and gospel fields, but had only found international acclaim after his show-stopping appearance at the Newport Jazz Festival in 1964. Happily, cover versions of his songs by the likes of folk-singers Peter, Paul and Mary had allowed this former sharecropper's son from South Carolina, who doubled as a preacher, to live his final years in comparative luxury.

Kamikaze Killers Massacre 25 After Paras Outwit Tel Aviv Hijackers

WHEN A CRACK TEAM of Israeli paratroopers dramatically ended the 23-hour hijacking of a Sabena Airlines plane at Lod International Airport in Tel Aviv today, the unlikely hero of the drama turned out to be a Belgian flight engineer. Unknown to Black September guerrillas who were holding the jet hostage, the engineer understood Arabic and was able to pass on their plans – in Flemish – to the control tower. Two hijackers were shot in the rescue operation and only two of the 92 passengers were injured.

Israeli relief and celebrations were tragically cut short on May 30 when three members of the Japanese Red Army, trained in Lebanon by the Popular Front for the Liberation of Palestine, opened fire in the crowded Lod Airport concourse and massacred 26 civilians.

Twelve of those killed by the kamikaze guerrillas, who'd arrived in Tel Aviv on an Air France flight and took grenades and rifles from their baggage as it arrived on a carousel, were Puerto Rican pilgrims to the Holy Land. Two of the Japanese were shot and a third arrested in what was the most astonishing security breach in Israel's history.

UK TOP 10 SINGLES

1: Amazing Grace
- The Royal Scots Dragoon Guards
2: Could It Be Forever/Cherish
- David Cassidy
3: Come What May
- Vicky Leandros
4: A Thing Called Love
- Johnny Cash
5: Rocket Man
- Elton John
6: Metal Guru
- T Rex
7: Tumbling Dice
- The Rolling Stones
8: Radancer
- Marmalade
9: Run Run Run
- Jo Jo Gunne
10: Back Off Boogaloo
- Ringo Starr

Born this month:
16: Frank Strandli, Norwegian international football player

DEPARTURES

Died this month:
2: John Edgar Hoover, US FBI chief, aged 77 (*see main story*)
3: Les Harvey, UK rock musician (*Stone The Crows*) electrocuted, aged 25
22: Cecil Day Lewis, British Poet Laureate, novelist, aged 68; Dame Margaret Rutherford, British Academy Award-winning comedy character actress, big-screen detective Miss Marple (*Passport To Pimlico, Blithe Spirit, The Importance Of Being Earnest, The VIPs, Murder She Said, Murder Most Foul*, etc), aged 80
28: Edward, Duke of Windsor, former King Edward VIII (*see main story*)

MAY 28

Duke Of Windsor Dies

JUST TEN DAYS before his death today, the Duke of Windsor had met with his niece Queen Elizabeth (pictured) – something of a reconciliation after years of what had been a strained relationship between the Duke and the royal family. As Edward VIII, he had reigned for a brief 11 months in 1936, before abdicating the throne in a moving broadcast to the British people.

His decision to abdicate and 'marry the woman I love' – American divorcée Wallis Simpson – sadly put a gulf between the British people and the man who had previously shown sympathy and concern for their hardship during the Depression.

Although the Duke was appointed Governor of the Bahamas between 1940 and 1945, he and the woman who had caused his abdication subsequently moved to France and very rarely visited Britain.

The Duke's body would be flown to Britain for burial next month.

MAY 25

Britain Goes On Neighbour Watch

A new comedy series, *Love Thy Neighbour,* made its début in the British TV ratings in second place today, with a reported 8.1 million households tuning in to watch a controversial show about Eddie Booth, a white suburban bigot (played by Jack Smethurst) who had a black family move in next door to him.

Rudolph Walker and Nina Baden-Semper were the unfortunate targets of his racism, and the programme was slammed by the race relations lobby for reinforcing, rather than undermining, prejudicial attitudes. The British viewing public clearly loved it, however, and the show would run for the next four years with similar success.

MAY 16

Southern Race Warrior Wallace Shot

Governor George Wallace of Alabama was effectively put out of the running for the US presidency today by a lone gunman who fired five bullets at him from close range during a political rally in Maryland.

Ironically, Wallace - a man who had fought racial integration every step of the way in America's Deep South, and had once personally barred the main entrance of the University of Alabama to prevent the admission of two black students in defiance of President Kennedy's desegregation order – was shot by a white man, 21-year-old Arthur Bremer.

Three other people were also injured in the attack, which doctors in Washington said would leave the Governor paralysed from the waist down. His assailant would be judged insane and sentenced to a life in protective custody.

MAY 24

Glasgow Rangers Conquer Europe

A boisterous tartan-clad army of some 20,000 Glaswegians travelled to Barcelona to see Scottish soccer team Glasgow Rangers achieve their first big European honour by winning the European Cup-Winners' Cup this evening.

Rangers beat Moscow Dynamo 3-2, though the sight of fans pouring onto the pitch after each goal took the gloss off proceedings, as did a battle with Spanish police on the final whistle, in which one man died and 150 were injured.

A subsequent UEFA ban for two years - reduced to one on appeal - further dampened Rangers' joy at finally emulating eternal rivals Glasgow Celtic's 1967 European Cup win.

MAY 29

Nixon And Brezhnev Promise Not To Fight

A momentous day for East-West relations, saw President Richard Nixon and Soviet Communist Party leader Leonid Brezhnev sign a treaty which, while it acknowledged the basic differences between the US and the Soviet Union, pledged each of them to arms reduction aimed at reducing the dangers of nuclear war.

Mr Nixon, who was making the first visit to the USSR by a US President, also took the opportunity to address the Soviet Union's TV audience, telling them that if the arms race continued unchecked, there would be no winners, only losers and casualties.

JUNE

German Police Capture Terror Leader Meinhof

WEST GERMAN POLICE finally arrested the last remaining leader of the Red Army Faction - or Baader-Meinhof gang - today when Ulrike Meinhof was brought into custody in Hanover, two weeks after Andreas Baader and two other gang members lost a gun battle with police in Frankfurt.

In the 1950s Meinhof, a respected 38-year-old left-wing television journalist, had campaigned vehemently, but peaceably, for a nuclear-free Germany. She was converted to the use of violence as the only means of effecting social change after interviewing Baader, who was then serving a prison sentence for arson.

In the preceding few weeks alone, the faction's war against German 'materialism' had resulted in four deaths and many serious injuries. Meinhof would be found hanged in her cell in 1976, with Baader committing suicide the following year, aged only 34, after being sentenced to life imprisonment.

Royal Family Buries Duke At Windsor

The Duke of Windsor was buried in a private ceremony today, his funeral attended only by members of the royal family and his wife, the woman he gave up his throne to marry in 1936.

Thousands of people had been able to view the Duke's coffin as it lay in state in St George's Chapel, Windsor, a sheaf of white lilies from the 75-year-old Duchess its only decoration. She, the Queen and the Duke of Edinburgh were screened off from the rest of the congregation during the funeral service.

The Duke was buried in Frogmore, close to a garden in which he had played as a child. After the service, the Duchess left for Heathrow Airport and returned to the home she and her husband had shared in Paris.

Democrats' Presidential Election HQ Burgled

Five men were arrested as they broke into the Democratic National Committee offices in the Watergate complex (pictured) in Washington DC tonight. Police believed that they had been intent on bugging the offices as they were found to be in possession of electronic surveillance equipment, walkie-talkies and cameras.

One of the men, James McCord, was said to be security coordinator for CREEP, the Committee to Re-elect the President, suggesting a campaign of dirty tricks in the race to the White House.

The Democrats were not slow to denounce what appeared to be Republican skulduggery and Hubert Humphrey, a candidate for nomination as Democratic contender for the presidency in November, demanded 'explanation and apology' from President Nixon. The Watergate Affair, as it was to become known, would eventually bring Nixon down in historic fashion, although firm denials from the White House would initially succeed in persuading the electorate to return Nixon to office.

UK TOP 10 SINGLES

1: Metal Guru
- T Rex
2: Vincent
- Don McLean
3: At The Club/Saturday Night At The Movies
- The Drifters
4: Lady Eleanor
- Lindisfarne
5: Oh Babe What Would You Say
- Hurricane Smith
6: California Man
- The Move
7: Rocket Man
- Elton John
8: Rockin' Robin
- Michael Jackson
9: Take Me Bak 'Ome
- Slade
10: Sister Jane
- New World

Blues Singer Jimmy Rushing Dies

Jimmy Rushing, best known for his spell fronting the Count Basie Band in the 1930s, died today in New York at the age of 69 following a short illness. Known as 'Mr Five By Five' due to his swelling girth, his voice earned the unique description of 'steel-bright in its upper range and, at its best, silky smooth' from novelist Ralph Ellison.

Born in August 1902, Rushing 'retired' when Basie broke up his first band in 1950, but would later form his own group. A trouper to the last, he was still fulfilling weekend singing engagements at New York's Half Note Club right up to his death.

JUNE 18

Britain Stunned By Worst-Ever Air Crash

IN THE WORST aviation disaster in UK history, 118 people died today when a BEA Trident bound for Brussels crashed shortly after taking off from London's Heathrow Airport. The plane was full to capacity following a last-minute rush by passengers to beat a proposed pilots' strike due to start the following day.

Early reports indicated that the tail broke loose from the plane, which immediately plummeted to earth. Although two people were rescued alive from the mangled wreckage, they later died in hospital. A Catholic priest was reported to have administered the last rites to about 60 victims.

The three-engined Hawker Siddeley Trident had hitherto enjoyed a good safety record, though it had been eclipsed in the sales stakes by Boeing's very similar 727.

JUNE 20

Bridge Goes Way Of Billy Joe

The Tallahatchie Bridge, immortalized in song by country music singer-songwriter Bobbie Gentry in her 1967 hit *Ode To Billy Joe*, collapsed today in Mississippi.

The song, which also inspired a book and a 1976 film, as well as winning its writer three Grammy Awards, told the tragic tale of one Billy Joe McAllister who took his own life by jumping off the said bridge, which spanned the Tallahatchie River west of Bobbie Gentry's birthplace in Chickasaw County, Mississippi.

JUNE 22

Provos Agree To Cease-Fire

A ray of hope appeared to cut through the gloom of Ulster politics today when William Whitelaw, the Northern Ireland Secretary, announced that the British Government would 'reciprocate' in unspecified fashion if the Provisional IRA did honour its offer to suspend operations in a few days' time.

Although there appeared to be the prospect of meaningful talks between the major players in the province's conflict, by June 30 Protestant hard-liners had begun building barricades in Belfast - a direct challenge to the rule of law enforced by British forces.

JUNE 19

Skyjacking On The Increase

The incidence of skyjacking, the aerial form of hijacking, had risen to such heights that pilots working for the commercial airlines finally called 'enough' today. Pilots from over 30 countries throughout the world staged a strike lasting several days which brought European airports to a virtual standstill.

For some, skyjacking was a means to political ends, while for others - such as the man who parachuted from an American Airlines jet over Indiana with a spade and $502,000 on June 24 - it was purely a money-making exercise.

JUNE

29

TINY OLGA AND MIGHTY MARK STAR IN MUNICH TERROR OLYMPICS

It's a source of wonder that the 1972 Munich Olympics, so cruelly hit by the Black September guerrilla massacre of Israeli athletes on September 5 (*see news pages*), not only went ahead but that so many of the young and gifted people who took part were able to cut off from the horror of those opening days and produce the often outstanding performances they did.

But the Games will forever be remembered for the impact and achievements of two in particular - the-17 year-old Russian gymnast Olga Korbut and Mark Spitz, the record-shattering 22-year-old Californian swimmer.

The art of gymnastics took on a new lease of life when the tiny Olga - only selected as a Russian team reserve - appeared at centre stage to capture the hearts and imaginations of viewers around the world with her innovative, daring and stylish routines.

She won gold for her pixie-like floor routine and gold again on the beam, adding a silver medal for her brilliant performance on the uneven parallel bars where she became the first person ever to perform a backwards somersault. Not surprisingly, she also picked up a gold as member of the winning Russian team. After marrying a Russian rock singer, Olga would later relocate to the US where she became a gymnastics teacher.

Mark Spitz ensured that swimming took its turn in the spotlight by taking a record seven gold medals in individual and team events in the Olympic pool. He powered to record-breaking victory in the freestyle and the butterfly over both 100 and 200 metres, and was a member of the US teams which won the 4 x 100m freestyle, the 4 x 200m and the 4 x 100m medley relays.

It was the absolute pinnacle of a remarkable five-year period (1967-72) in which Spitz set 26 world records in individual events and a further six as a relay team member. Capitalizing on his Munich achievements, Mark Spitz was able to become a successful businessman, unwisely - and unsuccessfully - attempting a comeback in 1992, only to be beaten by swimmers half his age.

On the Olympic track, US domination of the sprints was briefly ended by the 100m and 200m double gold of Russia's Valeri Borzov, although the US 4 x 100m relay team revenged that by beating the Russians into second place.

Lasse Viren - the brilliant Finnish runner - achieved the formidable 5,000m and 10,000m double, while Kenya's Kip Keino, the 1968 Mexico Games 1500m gold medallist and 5,000m silver winner, stepped up a discipline for Munich to take on the gruelling 3,000m steeplechase, which he duly won.

East Germany's Renate Stecher carried off the women's

sprint double, although she had to be content with a silver for the 4 x 100m relay which was won, to the obvious delight of the huge home crowd, by West Germany.

Medals were in short supply for British athletes, although David Hemery did win a bronze in the 400m hurdles, the event he'd won in Mexico '68, and the redoubtable Northern Ireland all-rounder Mary Peters - making her third Olympics appearance in the pentathlon - finally got her hands on the long-hunted gold medal when she beat West German Heide Rosendahl and East German Burglinde Pollack in a memorable and close-fought struggle.

There were medals too for British horsemen and women, with Richard Meade winning gold in the three day event individual contest, Britain taking the team gold in the same event and Ann Moore winning silver in the Grand Prix Jumping competition.

Despite everything, Munich '72 had proved a memorable two weeks of often breathtaking brilliance and superlatives.

Olga Korbut

JULY 1

Presidential Adviser In Marital Ultimatum

PRESIDENT NIXON'S election campaign manager, former Attorney-General John Mitchell, announced his resignation today saying that his wife had given him an ultimatum, either he quit politics or their marriage was over. Martha Mitchell had recently gone public on the state of their relationship, with the result that Nixon was to lose one of his closest advisers and confidants.

As the truth of Watergate unfolded in 1973, it transpired that Mitchell had not quit in time to prevent being charged with, and eventually jailed for, his part in the scandal.

And while his resignation didn't save his political skin, neither did it prevent his marriage collapsing when he and his wife were forced to spend all their time together. In September 1973, Martha Mitchell reported that he had walked out on her, adding that she was not sorry. 'I've been trying to get him out,' she claimed. 'I couldn't stand it. He was watching the football games!'

JULY 17

Bad Boy Fischer Takes World Chess Crown

American chess player Bobby Fischer, 29, today became the first non-Soviet player since 1948 to contest a world championship when he opened his series of games against reigning champion Boris Spassky in Reykjavik, capital of Iceland.

The US champion, who'd held his title since the age of 15, demanded a special chair, complained about the chessboard's colour and refused to show for the second game because the TV cameras were upsetting him – yet secured victory through his aggressive play and superior strategy.

Fischer won seven games to the Russian's two to take the title, but was unable to sustain his success and in 1975 lost the title by default when he failed to agree on conditions of play for a match with Anatoly Karpov. Nevertheless, his actions attracted great publicity for the game – publicity that remained unparalleled until Britain's Nigel Short challenged Garry Kasparov over two decades later.

Donny Osmond (seen with his family) - No 1 in the singles chart with *Puppy Love*

Egypt Rejects Soviet Aid

In a move calculated to improve relations with the West, Egyptian President Anwar Sadat today ordered the withdrawal of all Soviet military advisers from his country. There were thought to be around 5,000 military experts and nearly three times as many Soviet troops in Egypt, although it was unclear whether the order also applied to the latter.

President Sadat also announced full Egyptian control over military gains made during the Six-Day War with Israel in 1967.

JULY 1

'Hair' Cut – Few Distressed

Hair, the play that embodied the essence of sixties counter-culture with its mixture of songs, slogans and nudity, closed today after a four-year Broadway run, its pertinence and potency considered long-exhausted. Adapted from a book by Gerome Ragniu and James Rado, with music by Galt MacDermot, it told the story of an Oklahoman on the way to enlist for service in Vietnam who falls in with hippie 'flower people'. The show included songs that provided hits for The Fifth Dimension (*Aquarius/Let The Sunshine In*), The Cowsills (*Hair*) and Oliver (*Good Morning Starshine*), while a film version in 1979 proved too belated to make an impression, even as a curio.

UK TOP 10 SINGLES

1: Puppy Love
- Donny Osmond
2: Rock & Roll Part 2
- Gary Glitter
3: Take Me Back 'Ome
- Slade
4: Little Willie
- Sweet
5: Circles
- The New Seekers
6: Sylvia's Mother
- Dr Hook
7: I Can See Clearly Now
- Johnny Nash
8: An American Trilogy
- Elvis Presley
9: Vincent
- Don McLean
10: Rockin' Robin
- Michael Jackson

JULY 18

Home Secretary Maudling Resigns Over Poulson Link

ALLEGATIONS LINKING the British Home Secretary Reginald Maudling to the so called 'Poulson Affair' effectively put an end to his ministerial career today, when he offered his resignation to Prime Minister Edward Heath. A bankruptcy hearing involving top civic architect John Poulson had recently heard a series of allegations involving corruption of public servants, which had prompted a police inquiry into Poulson's business relationships.

Maudling, it was revealed, was an unpaid chairman of one of Poulson's companies, although his children received financial benefits as a result, and the ex-Home Secretary rented a large country house from another Poulson company at a peppercorn rent.

All this set up a clear conflict of loyalties with his position at the Home Office, which included ministerial responsibility for British police forces. Poulson would eventually be jailed for corruption, while Maudling remained a back bench Member of Parliament until his death in 1979.

JULY 31

McGovern Wins Democrat Nomination But Loses Running Mate

Just two and a half weeks after the McGovern-Eagleton ticket won the Democratic Party's nomination for this year's presidential election, Senator Thomas Eagleton resigned as vice-presidential running mate after an admission that he had twice received shock treatment for depression.

The revelations, and subsequent resignation of Eagleton, made something of a fool of George McGovern. He had recently and repeatedly stressed his support for Eagleton by saying he was '1,000 per cent' behind the Missouri senator.

But with mounting press speculation about his running mate's state of physical and mental health, McGovern was forced to ask the 42-year-old Eagleton to go. He would be replaced in August by Sargent Shriver, the late President John Kennedy's brother-in-law.

Stones Gather Much Fuss

The Rolling Stones' North American tour rolled on today, despite a bomb which blew out the cones of 30 speakers on an equipment truck in Montreal. 'Why didn't that cat leave a note?' mused a jocular Mick Jagger before going on stage as usual.

A week later, the band would play New York's Madison Square Garden to an audience of 20,000, having meanwhile suffered five arrests at Warwick, Rhode Island, after a disagreement with a photographer.

Jagger and guitarist Keith Richards were among those involved in the incident, which caused a four-hour delay to the group's Boston show that night.

Sutch Is Life!

David Sutch, better known as Screaming Lord Sutch the rock 'n' roll star, was arrested today after a publicity stunt in London to mark his move into British politics.
Accompanied by four naked women, he leapt from a bus opposite Downing Street - location of the Prime Minister's official residence - to alert Mr Heath (and the waiting media) to a forthcoming fund-raising concert.
Charges of insulting behaviour would be dismissed, though Sutch would later form the Monster Raving Loony Party and stand in innumerable by-elections.

JULY

AUGUST 26

World-Girdler Chichester Dies

The English adventurer and yachtsman, Sir Francis Chichester, died today at the age of 70. Born in Barnstaple, Devon, he spent almost 50 years triumphing over adversity - starting in the late 1920s, when he flew a *Gipsy Moth* biplane solo to Australia, and surviving serious injury only two years later when the plane he was piloting crashed in Japan.

In the 1950s his relish for adventure inspired him to take up yacht-racing, but in 1957 he was told he had lung cancer. Determined to beat the disease, which he did, Chichester proved his resilience by winning the 1960 solo transatlantic yacht race in his boat *Gipsy Moth III*.

However, he will be best remembered for his record-breaking non-stop solo round-the-world voyage of 1966-7, a trip which he completed in 226 days in the 54-foot ketch *Gipsy Moth IV*. Knighted for his achievement, Sir Francis recounted his nautical adventures engagingly in his books T*he Lonely Sea And The Sky* and *Gipsy Moth Circles The World*.

AUGUST 12

This Alice Is No Lady!

The British charts were shaken to their foundations this month by the arrival of US shock-rocker Alice Cooper. Real name Vincent Furnier and the son of a clergyman, his snake-toting, doll-beheading act was guaranteed to stir up outrage, while *School's Out* - a rebellious anthem released to coincide with the summer vacation - scaled the heights to become the UK's No 1 single for three weeks.

Cooper's fame was accentuated during one visit to Britain when the old lady sitting next to him on the flight to London was found to have died, of natural causes, in her sleep. Cooper later mock-regretted he'd not thought to make fake fang-marks in her neck!

Uganda's Amin Expels 50,000 Asians

UGANDA'S INCREASINGLY erratic dictator, General Idi Amin, astounded the British Government and the world today by announcing his intention of expelling all 50,000 Asians in the country who held British passports.

Speaking from the Ugandan capital, Kampala, Amin accused the Asian community - some of whose families had settled in East Africa 100 years earlier to start forming Uganda's most successful and prosperous ethnic group of 'sabotaging the economy'. Observers suggested the Asians had simply turned out to be the largest number of scapegoats available for a man whose nation was in dire financial straits.

Amin's move was not without its advantages for many of the Asians victimized. Instead of waiting patiently for a place in the queue of thousands wanting to enter Britain each year, they could now claim asylum from the tyrant's brutal regime and crumbling empire.

UK TOP 10 SINGLES

1: School's Out
- Alice Cooper

2: Seaside Shuffle
- Terry Dactyl & The Dinosaurs

3: Puppy Love
- Donny Osmond

4: Silver Machine
- Hawkwind

5: Breaking Up Is Hard To Do
- The Partridge Family

6: Popcorn
- Hot Butter

7: Sylvia's Mother
- Dr Hook

8: Rock & Roll Part 2
- Gary Glitter

9: I Can See Clearly Now
- Johnny Nash

10: You Wear It Well
- Rod Stewart

ARRIVALS

Born this month:
7: Phil Whelan, England Under-21 international football player
8: Steven Tweed, Scotland Under-21 international football player
14: Karl Ready, Wales Under-21 international football player

DEPARTURES

Died this month:
2: Brian Cole, US pop musician, singer (*The Association*), aged 29
29: Lale Andersen, German popular singer, originator of *Lili Marlene*, aged 67

AUGUST 11

US Withdraws Troops From Vietnam

TODAY MARKED THE END of US involvement on the ground in the Vietnam War, more than seven years after the first marines set foot on South Vietnamese soil in what was then described as 'a purely defensive role'. That defensive role turned into an offensive one only days later when the marines were sent into action against North Vietnamese Vietcong forces to begin a war which would cost the lives of 45,000 US servicemen.

Although the pull-out of the 3rd Battalion of the 21st US Infantry from Da Nang honoured President Nixon's 1971 pledge to end US involvement in South Vietnam, there was to be no let-up in the heavy bombing being inflicted by the USAF's B-52 bombers on strategic targets in North Vietnam.

Increased air activity wreaked havoc on the ground, though there was doubt in some quarters about its effectiveness – the Vietcong in Quangtri province had so far been successful in keeping their heavy artillery well-hidden from US observers and safe from US bombs.

AUGUST 3

Unions Delay Texan Clydebank Rescue Deal

Texan millionaire Wayne Harbin, president of Marathon Manufacturing, the company involved in talks to save Glasgow's Upper Clyde Shipbuilders (UCS) by creating more than 2,000 jobs building oil rigs and platforms, threatened to pull out of the deal today unless the boilermakers' union agreed to an arbitration clause within a few more days.

Ironically, the union involved was headed by Danny McGarvey, who had contacted Mr Harbin with the idea of saving UCS when it collapsed with debts of £17 million ($35m). Marathon Manufacturing would eventually go through with the rescue package, but not until October.

Jane Fonda In The Wars

Despite the fact that US ground troops had pulled out of Vietnam this month, the continued US bombing raids meant that anti-war demonstrations in the US also carried on. Nixon's appeal to the 'silent majority' - those who were assumed to support their government's stance on Vietnam - failed to make any impact on demonstrators in Miami today, where 900 were arrested by police as violence erupted.

One of the most notable and vociferous celebrities to support the anti-war movement was Jane Fonda (pictured), daughter of actor Henry, who this month accused the US of bombing dikes in the Hanoi region. Active in the peace movement since the late 1960s, the Oscar-winning actress was vilified then for travelling to North Vietnam to make the film documentary *Introduction To The Enemy*.

Replying to Fonda's allegations, America's First Lady, Pat Nixon, denounced her in Washington this month, saying that she 'should ask her friends in Hanoi to stop their aggression'.

Lennons Give Charity A Chance

John Lennon and Yoko Ono today played their first official American concert - a benefit for New York's Willowbrook Hospital, at Madison Square Garden - on a bill which they shared with Motown star Stevie Wonder and rock revivalists Sha Na Na.

Backed by a group called Elephant's Memory, the couple played an 18-song set that included four songs sung by Yoko, a version of The Beatles' *Come Together* and a cover of Elvis Presley's *Hound Dog*. Their appearance was, perhaps inevitably, climaxed by the Lennon anthem Give *Peace A Chance*.

DAVID CASSIDY - KEEPING IT IN THE FAMILY

The decision to launch David Cassidy as a solo star in Britain this summer was a master-stroke by his managers and record company which would signal the arrival of a teen idol only Donny Osmond could match in terms of chart success and box-office appeal - and he had the benefit of his equally successful brothers to bolster his career.

David Cassidy had been a team player too in the US where, as a member of the hugely-popular *The Partridge Family* sit-com TV series and recording group, the 22-year-old's personal popularity had - in 1970 - helped the single *I Think I Love You* sell more than five million copies. Despite the series not being shown in Britain, the single had also become a No 18 British chart hit.

A couple more Cassidy-led *Partridge Family* singles had done well in 1971, so it was inevitable that an official David Cassidy solo single would be released before long. In the US, that happened last October with a reworking of the Association hit *Cherish*. By December it was fixed in the US Top 10 and had passed the million sales mark.

The arrival of the US TV series on British screens, the success of *The Partridge Family* single *It's One Of Those Nights* and the flurry of intense interest shown in young Mr Cassidy by British teen magazines led to the release of a double A-sided *Could It Be Forever/Cherish,* a 17-week chart run with a peak of No 2.

His immense popularity in the US was reflected in the appearance, on May 11, of a *Rolling Stone* magazine cover feature, with a bare-chested Cassidy looming out of US news-stands. In Britain, the roll continued through 1972 with a September No 1 hit (*How Can I Be Sure*) and a relatively unsuccessful No 11 (*Rock Me Baby*) in November.

Through the next two years, David Cassidy would biff it

out with Donny Osmond, score five more huge hits (including the October 1973 No 1 *Daydreamer/The Puppy Song*) before deciding to return to his acting career on TV, films and the US musical stage.

OLIVIA - TOOMORROW, THE WORLD!

One of the most unlikely international success stories of the 1970s began last March with the first British hit by a young girl singer whose grandfather was a Nobel Prize-winning Cambridge University scientist, who'd been raised in Australia from the age of five, returned to England as one half of a folk-singing duo, was snapped up to be one of a group of sci-fi teenagers in a futuristic sequel to The Monkees, became one of the biggest-selling acts in US country music with records made in London's Abbey Road Studios, and ended the decade as a movie star singing a pastiche of 1950s' rock 'n' roll.

Olivia Newton-John was 24 when this year began, had already completed work on *Toomorrow,* the flop sci-fi musical comedy movie US producer Don Kirshner - inventor of The Monkees - had funded with a view to creating a hit TV series, duetted with Cliff Richard (whose manager was also her manager) on the B-side of his hit *Sunny Honey Girl,* and was living with Bruce Welch, rhythm guitarist of The Shadows, top British instrumental combo and Cliff's regular backing team.

In March 1971, her cover version of Bob Dylan's *If Not For You* and the traditional *Banks Of The Ohio* (arranged by Welch and co-producer John Farrer) had begun a string of international hits which would find special favour with US country music fans.

And while this year was quiet as far as the charts were concerned (with only *What Is Life* reaching the British Top 20), Olivia was about to blossom internationally.

Between 1973 (when her cover of John Denver's *Take Me Home Country Roads* gave Olivia her first US No 1) and 1978, pretty well everything she recorded would make the US country Top 10 chart and sell a million. In 1976 she won the ultimate accolade when the Country Music Association voted her Female Artist of the Year, beating the likes of Dolly Parton and Tammy Wynette.

In 1978, Olivia would co-star with John Travolta in the hit movie *Grease,* change direction to a more sophisticated disco-type feel and head into the 1980s as one of the world's hottest acts.

THREE DOG STAY HOT IN '72

Destined to be the ninth most successful US singles act of the 1970s, the California-based Three Dog Night this year continued the roll begun in 1969 with their version of Otis Redding's *Try A Little Tenderness,* highlighted in 1970 with *Mama Told Me (Not To Come)* and 1971 with *Joy To The World,* with four multi million sellers.

Like everything they recorded, none of their 1972 hits – *Never Been To Spain, The Family Of Man, Black And White* and *Pieces Of April* – was written by them. The group, a seven-piece fronted by three singers, Danny Hutton, Cory Wells and Chuck Negron, had been put together with the aim of creating an outfit which could play exceptionally well in a variety of styles and draw entirely on the material of proven hit songwriters.

It was a formula which succeeded incredibly well and, during their peak years of 1969-74, would result in 16 million-selling US hit singles and seven gold or platinum award-winning albums.

Strangely, although the group did tour Europe in 1971 to win a fair degree of critical and audience enthusiasm, only

Olivia Newton-John

two of their US monster hits – *Mama Told Me (Not To Come)* and *Joy To The World* – would give them any chart success in Britain or Europe.

Sadly, and almost inevitably, Three Dog Night's last album before the original line-up went their separate ways – the ironically titled *Hard Labor* – was recorded in 1974 amid such acrimony that vocal tracks were recorded in different sessions because the singers couldn't bear to be in the same room together!

SEPT

Black September Guerrillas Massacre Israeli Olympians

IN AN ATROCITY that cast a terrible shadow over the Munich Olympic Games, 11 Israeli athletes were today gunned down - two of them in the Olympic Village when Black September terrorists stormed the Israeli compound, the others on the Tarmac of Furstenfeld military airport when a West German police plan to rescue them from being taken, as hostages, onto a waiting aircraft, went horribly wrong.

The tragedy began at 5.10 am when the Black September guerrillas scaled the compound fence and burst into the dormitories, firing indiscriminately with sub-machine-guns. Two athletes were killed outright and nine taken hostage. Many more athletes had made their escape when the alarm was sounded.

By midday, when the Village was surrounded by 12,000 armed police, the guerrillas made their demands known – they wanted the release of 200 Palestinians held in Israeli jails, and their own safe passage out of Munich.

Although the Israeli Government steadfastly refused to free any prisoners, by the end of the day the West Germans had apparently agreed to allow the kidnappers to leave with their hostages. The terrorists, under the impression they were flying to a Middle Eastern country, were taken by helicopter to the military airfield outside Munich.

Later, when they left the helicopter to transfer to a jet, German marksmen opened fire. The rescue attempt failed, however, as all nine Israeli hostages died in the gun battle. Four of the terrorists also perished, as did one police officer.

Israeli athletes who had escaped the initial attack packed their bags and left the Games because of what they believed to be inadequate security.

Nixon Aides Charged With Watergate Break-In

Two of President Nixon's former White House aides - Howard Hunt and G Gordon Liddy - were among seven men indicted by a Washington court today and charged with conspiring to break into the Democratic Party headquarters in Watergate on June 17.

Before working for Nixon's re-election campaign, Liddy was a presidential assistant, while Hunt's background included a period with the CIA. The White House continued to deny any knowledge of, or complicity in, the burglary, saying there was 'absolutely no evidence' that any other White House personnel were involved.

Britain's Youth Crave Cassidy

Pre-pubescent mania gripped Britain this month as top US teen idol David Cassidy registered his first No 1 with *How Can I Be Sure*. A cover of a Young Rascals hit from 1967, it captivated a huge audience who couldn't have known that Cassidy's career in the States was already on the slide.

A *Rolling Stone* interview in March this year had reported Cassidy's dissatisfaction with his 'squeaky-clean' image as Keith Partridge of the made for-TV group The Partridge Family, which, though dead and buried in the US, was still doing well in Britain.

Cassidy would enjoy another UK chart-topper in late 1973 with *Daydreamer/The Puppy Song* before fading from view like so many pin-ups before and since – though he resurfaced in the 1990s with his younger brother Shaun and Petula Clark in the US stage production of Willy Russell's *Blood Brothers*.

My Lai Massacre Inquiry Ends

A sorry chapter in the US' involvement in the Vietnam War ended today when the US Army finalized its inquiry into the My Lai Massacre. In total, 13 officers and conscripts were initially charged with the wholesale slaughter in 1968 of 109 inhabitants of the South Vietnamese village of that name, but only their commander, Lieutenant William Calley, was found to be guilty.

Calley was sentenced to life imprisonment, a term which was subsequently reduced to ten years by the direct intervention of President Nixon. Held in jail since being found guilty after his part in a court martial in 1971, Calley would be paroled in 1974.

UK TOP 10 SINGLES

1: Mama Weer All Crazee Now
- Slade
2: You Wear It Well
- Rod Stewart
3: It's Four In The Morning
- Faron Young
4: Sugar Me
- Lyndsey De Paul
5: Virginia Plain
- Roxy Music
6: Standing In The Road
- Blackfoot Sue
7: All The Young Dudes
- Mott The Hoople
8: How Can I Be Sure
- David Cassidy
9: I Get The Sweetest Feeling
- Jackie Wilson
10: Children Of The Revolution
- T Rex

ARRIVALS
Born this month:
6: Brian O'Neil, Scotland Under-21 international football player
26: Alan Neilson, Welsh football player

DEPARTURES
Died this month:
14: Geoffrey Francis Fisher (Lord Fisher of Lambeth), Archbishop of Canterbury 1945-61, aged 75
18: Ian Smith, Scottish international Rugby Union player (32 caps 1924-33, captain 1933, British Lions player)
27: Rory Storm (Alan Caldwell), UK pop singer (*Rory Storm & The Hurricanes*)

Amin Praises Hitler As Asians Run Terror Gauntlet

THE BIZARRE BEHAVIOUR of Ugandan dictator Idi Amin (pictured) was proving to be increasingly bad for his country's economy. The US today withdrew a $3 million loan to Uganda after Amin publicly praised Hitler amid the continued expulsion of thousands of Asians and other foreign nationals, including a number of US citizens.

It was reported that the Ugandan Army, which Amin had decreed to be above the law, was mounting roadblocks around Kampala Airport, relieving the fleeing Asians of everything of value. Those who did escape said they'd been bullied and beaten, and many more Asians were said to be stranded in the capital, afraid to run the gauntlet.

Amazingly, some people were actually trying to get *into* the country – but the Ugandans had repulsed an 'invasion' of Tanzanian refugees who tried to cross the border on September 18!

SEPTEMBER 16

Jimmy Hill On The Line

BBC TV soccer commentator Jimmy Hill temporarily abandoned his post today when an official at Arsenal's game with Liverpool at Highbury Stadium, North London, sustained an injury. When the referee appealed in vain for a qualified linesman over the public address system, Hill – a former professional player before becoming manager of Coventry City – changed into a track suit and took up the flag.

When highlights of the game were broadcast the following day on *The Big Match*, Hill had the luxury of reviewing his own decisions – something he admitted the partisan Highbury crowd had not been slow to do at the time!

SEPTEMBER 26

Heath Pleads For Pay Restraint

Fresh from talks with Trades Union Congress leader Vic Feather, when he was known to have proposed a radical voluntary prices and incomes policy to help curb galloping inflation, Prime Minister Edward Heath tonight appealed to British workers to limit future pay rises to no more than £2 ($5) a week, and manufacturers not to raise prices of goods more than 5 per cent.

Speaking at London's Press Club, Mr Heath said, 'We are not prepared to allow inflation to take control of events'.

The PM's appeal came in the knowledge that miners were already demanding rises between £4.50 ($10) and £7 ($16), power workers had a £5.50 ($12) increase in mind, while dustmen were asking for £4 ($9) a week more.

SEPTEMBER 28

'War And Peace' Hits UK TV Screens

The product of three years' work finally made it onto British television tonight when the first part of *War And Peace* - the BBC's adaptation of Tolstoy's epic novel - was broadcast. Its stars included Rupert Davies (as Count Rostov), Morag Hood (as Natasha), Faith Brook (as Countess Rostova), Alan Dobie (as Andrei Bolkonsky) and Anthony Hopkins (as Pierre). Location filming in Yugoslavia, combined with special effects work at Television Centre, went to produce a landmark in television drama. Its 20 episodes were screened weekly, ending in February 1973. Some two decades later, when it was finally releas-ed on video, Hopkins was enjoying unprecedented fame - and an Academy Award - as the psychopath Hannibal Lecter in *Silence Of The Lambs*.

British Money To Go Decimal?

The first shots in the war to drag Britain's archaic and complex money system into line with almost all the world were fired in London today with the publication of a Royal Mint report which suggested that it would be sensible for the currency to go decimal.

At present, British schoolchildren had to come to grips with a currency which had four farthings to the penny, 12 pennies to the shilling and 20 shillings to the pound, with all kinds of twiddly extras (like the half-crown, which was 30 pence, and the guinea, which was one pound and one shilling) to muddy the mental waters even further and make maths tests a sadist's delight in the setting.

Chuck's Chart-Topper Rings Bell

Chuck Berry, the veteran rock 'n' roller who first achieved fame in the 1950s, scored his first transatlantic chart-topper this month - not with one of his many rock classics, however, but with a novelty song, *My Ding-A-Ling*.

A nursery-rhyme styled crowd-participation number recorded live in Britain, at the Lanchester Arts Festival, *My Ding-A-Ling* received sales-boosting notoriety when UK moral guardian Mary Whitehouse called unsuccessfully for an airwave ban because of the song's supposed obscenity.

Berry, of course, revelled in the *double entendre* – and the resulting royalties for a song he had actually recorded in 1958 as the euphemistically titled *My Tambourine*.

SALT Agreement Signed In Washington

THE FIRST STRATEGIC ARMS LIMITATION TREATY (SALT) was signed today in the White House by Soviet Foreign Minister Andrei Gromyko and President Richard Nixon. Hailed by the Russians as 'a significant achievement in restraining the arms race', SALT prohibited either country from producing more intercontinental ballistic missiles (ICBMs) for the next five years.

The Soviet Union currently possessed half as many missiles again as the United States, although this was offset by America's possession of more multi-warhead missiles.

Negotiated ultimately during Nixon's summit meeting with Soviet leader Leonid Brezhnev in Moscow six months previously, SALT would prove an eve-of-election public relations triumph for the US President, who managed to enhance his new-found image as an international statesman by announcing that the US and USSR were to have a new round of arms limitation talks in Geneva. Even those who were cynical about the timing of today's ceremony had to admit SALT was a major achievement of the *détente* process pursued by Mr Nixon. A second SALT would be negotiated and signed in the late 1970s, imposing even further limitations on both sides.

OCTOBER 10

Betjeman Is New Poet Laureate

John Betjeman today succeeded Cecil Day Lewis as the British Poet Laureate in what was universally hailed as a popular choice.

Although many regarded Betjeman's poetry as lightweight, it was undeniably witty and evocative, with a strong sense of the spirit of place and a slightly melancholic undertone which gave it wide appeal. At the same time he maintained a sensitivity to social nuance which raised many a smile, also raising his work above the level of mere nostalgia.

In his capacity as Poet Laureate, Betjeman would write such verses as *14 November 1973,* on the occasion of Princess Anne's wedding to Captain Mark Phillips, but he was not entirely happy with his 'official' output, which was certainly not representative of his best work.

ARRIVALS

Born this month:
5: Darren Bazeley, England Under-21 international football player
6: Mark Skilling, Scotland Under-21 international football player
27: Lee Clark, England Under-21 international football player

DEPARTURES

Died this month:
1: Dr Louis Leakey, UK anthropologist and palaeontologist, aged 69 (*see Came & Went pages*)
17: Billy Williams, US pop singer (*The Pied Piper, I'm Gonna Sit Right Down And Write Myself A Letter,* etc), aged 55
24: Jackie Robinson, American baseball superstar, all-round athlete (Brooklyn Dodgers 1946-56), aged 53
31: Bill Durnan, Canadian icehockey goaltender (Montreal Canadiens 1944-50)

OCTOBER 16

Life On The Farm

EMMERDALE FARM, **DESTINED** to become one of British TV's best-loved soap operas, was broadcast for the first time today. It started life as undemanding lunchtime entertainment for housewives, who would stop their chores and enjoy a slice of country life from the imaginary village of Beckindale, Yorkshire, as they supped a cup of tea.

Sheila Mercier, an accomplished actress and sister of stage farce king Brian Rix, appeared in the first episode as Jacob Sugden's widow Annie, and would remain in the cast in the 1990s, the only original to survive many inevitable changes.

The programme dropped the 'Farm' from its title and, in the 1990s, added a raft of younger, streetwise characters to make the show more attractive to those who'd been wooed away by teen-led Australian imports.

Aviation Pioneer Sikorsky Dies

OCTOBER 26

Russian-American aviation entrepreneur Igor Sikorsky died today at the age of 83. Born in Kiev, he attended the Naval Academy at St Petersburg and Kiev Polytechnic before taking an engineering course in Paris. His first biplane designs, including the gigantic Ilia Mourumetz bomber, were used by the Russians in World War I, but it was after his defection to the West - following the Russian Revolution in 1917 - that Sikorsky came into his own.

After turning his attention to rotary-wing flight, he flew his prototype VS-300 in September 1939, so launching a successful series of helicopter designs that would revolutionize casualty evacuation warfare, air-sea rescue and many other aviation applications.

Although he officially retired in 1957, Sikorsky had remained a consultant to the company that bore his name, and had been in his Stratford, Connecticut, office the day before he died.

OCTOBER 22

Top Footballer Loses Eye And Career

The glittering career of Stoke City's England international goalkeeper Gordon Banks was effectively ended today, in a car crash, as he drove home after attending the club's Victoria Ground for routine treatment. Such was Banks's stature - he was one of the English team that won the 1966 World Cup - that British TV programmes were interrupted with reports on his progress in hospital as surgeons fought, unsuccessfully, to save his left eye.

Banks would never play competitive football again, but bowed out at the top after 251 appearances in the Stoke goal. One of his last games had been in the club's historic League Cup win against Chelsea at the end of last season – their first major prize in an 84-year history. He also won 73 England caps and was rated as one of the world's most outstanding goalkeepers of all time.

OCTOBER 26

Vietnam - 'Peace With Honour' Says Nixon

Continuing progress in the Paris Peace Conference on the Vietnam War was apparently in keeping with President Nixon's promise to attain 'peace with honour' rather than 'peace with surrender'. That was, if you chose to believe the President's statements today, as he toured southern states as part of his election campaign.

Not surprisingly, the Vietnam War was figuring large in the race to the White House and National Security Adviser Henry Kissinger, with brilliant timing, was claiming that one more round of talks at the Conference would produce a cease-fire agreement. Democratic Party candidate George McGovern said that while Mr Nixon would undoubtedly take credit, anti-war activists deserved the greatest praise.

MAY 2

J EDGAR HOOVER - THE REAL POWER BEHIND THE THRONE

It is true to say that while official expressions of regret at news of the death today of J Edgar Hoover - the man whose name was synonymous with America's FBI law enforcement agency for close on 50 years - were both fulsome and respectful, there were many who did not mourn his departure at the age of 77.

The simple truth was that Hoover had, for many years, used his considerable power base to exercise malevolent control over often very senior public figures with threats and blackmail only two of his most favoured weapons. Corrupted by power and certain that he was always right, he became a dangerously negative man.

Appointed Director of the FBI in 1924 – although at that time it was just the Bureau of Investigation, the 'Federal' was added in 1935 – Hoover's early years with the agency saw him vastly improve its efficiency and reputation, founding a training academy, pioneering many new crime-fighting techniques such as fingerprinting, and launching high-profile campaigns against leading criminals who became known as 'public enemies'.

During World War II, however, the FBI was asked to take on the role of protecting the United States from possible infiltration by enemy spies and it was this aspect of his work which the ultra-conservative Hoover tackled with the greatest zeal, continuing - during the Cold War period - to channel his energies and venom at those he personally considered to be communist subversives.

In Hoover's book, so-called liberals were as great a danger to the US as any card-carrying commies, and he abused his powers to wire-tap, 'bug' and otherwise target many such people, not least all three Kennedy brothers and civil rights leader Dr Martin Luther King. The FBI even had former Beatle John Lennon on its notorious 'enemies of the state' list!

It is a measure of his powerful position that, despite coming in for justified criticism for failing to break up organized crime (he steadfastly refused to acknowledge the existence of the Mafia for many years, making a mockery of the 'war' depicted in the TV series *The Untouchables*) and being accused of violating civil rights in the anti-leftwing purges of the 1950s, Hoover remained firmly in power throughout eight presidencies.

APRIL 27
KWAME NKRUMAH - THE HERO TURNED VILLAIN

Nobody better personifies the all-too-common African tragedy of rise to triumphant leadership of a newly-independent state and a fall from grace when the power of that leadership was abused than Kwame Nkrumah, who died today at the age of 63, exiled for the past six years from Ghana, the nation he had led to liberation in 1957.

Born in what was then the western Gold Coast, Nkrumah was educated at Lincoln University, Pennsylvania and the London School of Economics. Returning to the Gold Coast, he founded the Convention People's Party to seek self-government, won the general election of 1954 and was Prime Minister when the newly-named Ghana became a British dominion in 1957.

In 1960, when Ghana became a republic within the British Commonwealth, Nkrumah was the country's first President - and was then a well-respected member of the growing Pan-African union, supporting Nasser and the Arabs, showing consistent hostility to South Africa, but managing to remain politically neutral.

His rule at home became increasingly dictatorial, leading to his interference on a number of occasions, with the law itself. Personal and government extravagance, coupled with a slump in the world price of cocoa, Ghana's most important product, led to runaway inflation and economic chaos.

The end you probably know, but in February 1966 Nkrumah was on a state visit to China when the Ghanaian Army seized control. Unable to return home, Nkrumah spent some time in Guinea before travelling to Romania for medical treatment. It was there that he died, his country at least acknowledging its debt to him as a former national leader by according him a decent funeral at his birthplace in July.

OCTOBER 1
LOUIS LEAKEY - THE HISTORY MAN

It would be stretching a point to describe palaeontology - the study of life in the geological past - as a glamorous science. Certainly, it has always been less glamorous than, say, archaeology. That at least offers the opportunity for the discovery of something rare and beautiful, or mysterious.

Dr Louis Leakey, the British-born but Kenyan-naturalized scientist who died today at the age of 69, was a man trained in both disciplines, and it is true to say that his discoveries in the palaeontology field would prove every bit as enthralling and fascinating to the public as any previously unknown ruins or rare artefacts he and his wife Mary might have uncovered during their years investigating sites in Kenya's Olduvai Gorge.

They made their first significant fossil discoveries in the early 1930s, but it was in 1959 - when he unearthed the partial remains of what turned out to be the oldest-known (at that time) ancestor of Man - that Leakey became an international celebrity. Dating from about 1,750,000 years ago, and twice as old as any previous so-called 'missing link' between Man and apes, the remains he called 'Lucy' would gain the more proper scientific name of *Australopithecus boisei*.

Even though some members of the academic community quibbled about Leakey's interpretation of his fossils, the unscientific majority of us were simply stunned at so dramatic a discovery, even though Leakey himself did his best to tell us that he thought he'd found the remains of extinct hominids - that's primates to you - and not a direct ancestor of Man.

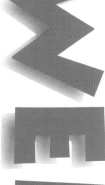

NOVEMBER 7

US Tries To Bomb North Vietnam Into Deal

US MILITARY LEADERS confirmed today that their hopes of peace in Vietnam were raised by the belief that recent increased bombing had damaged the North Vietnamese economy so badly, the Hanoi regime would be forced to agree a cease-fire settlement in the Paris talks.

'Even if the bombs don't coerce the enemy into successful peace talks, they're destroying his will to fight,' one senior US officer was reported as saying, echoing recent Washington suggestions that the US could win better peace terms than had been thought possible before the offensive intensified. As anti-war spokesmen in the US disputed this theory, it was confirmed that North Vietnamese air defences had shot down their first US B-52 bomber on November 22. Hanoi may have been battered, but it wasn't beaten yet.

NOVEMBER 1

Tragic Poet Ezra Pound Dies

American poet, critic and literary entrepreneur Ezra Pound died today at the age of 87. Born in Idaho, he travelled to Europe as a young man where he mixed with such literary greats as Yeats, Hemingway and Gertrude Stein. Settling in Italy in 1925, he began producing his most controversial work, *The Cantos*.

Caught up in the Fascist mood of 1930s and 1940s Italy, he made anti-democratic broadcasts in the early 1940s, which resulted in him being forcibly repatriated to the US at the end of the war to stand trial for treason.

In a chilling echo of the Soviet regime's treatment of dissidents, Pound was declared insane and put in an asylum, where he remained for 13 years. Despite his fall from grace and apparent descent into insanity, many – TS Eliot among them – regarded him as the motivating force behind modern poetry who, at his best, was a master craftsman of both traditional and modern verse forms.

NOVEMBER 6

Heath Imposes UK Wage And Price Freeze

The failure of the Trades Union Congress to negotiate voluntary pay curbs with the Confederation of British Industry - despite a mammoth 64-hour session at the conference table - prompted the government to introduce a 90-day freeze on wages, prices and rents today, with an option to extend the freeze for a further 60 days.

Backtracking on a promise to abandon former Prime Minister Harold Wilson's pay restraint policies, Conservative PM Edward Heath regretted that the decision had been necessary.

This was a regret shared by Tory rebels led by the outspoken Enoch Powell, who accused the PM of having 'taken leave of his senses'. Leading British employers, fearful of future strikes, quickly settled several large wage claims before the emergency legislation took effect. For instance, printers in Fleet Street, centre of the British newspaper publishing industry, were given an immediate 16 per cent increase.

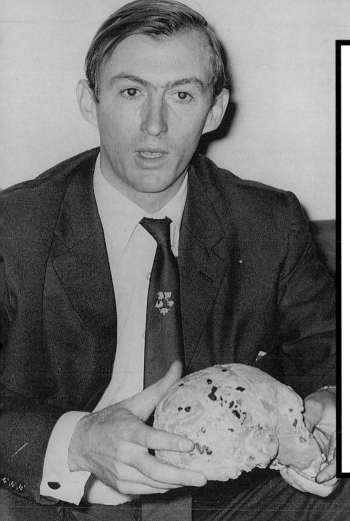

Leakey Jr Finds Oldest Human Skull

Not much more than a month after he buried his own father, the distinguished anthropologist Dr Louis Leakey, palaeontologist Richard Leakey revealed his latest find to the British media. The 2.6 million-year-old human skull, found by him at Lake Rudolf in Kenya, pushed back the origins of the human species by a million years and was the oldest so-called 'missing link' yet discovered.

Richard Leakey developed a passion for his profession very early in life, working alongside his father and mother, Mary Douglas Leakey – a formidable archaeologist in her own right – in his native Kenya and neighbouring Tanganyika.

UK TOP 10 SINGLES

1: Clair
- Gilbert O'Sullivan
2: Mouldy Old Dough
- Lieutenant Pigeon
3: Leader Of The Pack
- The Shangri-Las
4: Loop Di Love
- Shag
5: My Ding-A-Ling
- Chuck Berry
6: Donna
- 10cc
7: Elected
- Alice Cooper
8: In A Broken Dream
- Python Lee Jackson
9: Goodbye To Love
- The Carpenters
10: Crazy Horses
- The Osmonds

NOVEMBER 7

Nixon Romps To Landslide Victory

DEMOCRATIC PARTY PRESIDENTIAL CANDIDATE Senator George McGovern, the hope of millions of anti-war protesters and liberals, was tonight nursing his wounds after being severely beaten by the present incumbent of the White House, Richard Milhous Nixon (pictured).

Nixon's landslide victory left his opponent with only two wins - in the traditional Democrat heartland state of Massachusetts, and the District of Columbia - in a presidential election which had seen the lowest turnout of voters since the late 1940s. Only 55.7 per cent of those eligible bothered to take part.

As Nixon and Vice-President Spiro T Agnew were both elected to a second term of office, the President exhorted the American people to 'get on with the great tasks that lie before us'. George McGovern returned to the Senate, but would lose his seat in the 1980 election.

NOVEMBER 17

Court Gags Thalidomide Story

New evidence contained in a *Sunday Times* article about the drug thalidomide was suppressed by the High Court in London today, which ruled that the matter was still *sub judice* - unable to be reported or commented on as it was still the subject of a court hearing.

Later in the month Sir Keith Joseph, the UK Health Minister, announced that £3 million ($7m) of government money would go to help the disabled victims of the drug, stressing that this money was not intended to provide full compensation.

The legal battle against Distillers (UK), the company responsible for marketing thalidomide in the UK, was still raging and the government had indicated that more funds would be made available when the case was settled.

In December, Distillers (UK) made an offer of £11 million to those born severely handicapped after their mothers had used a drug designed to cure morning sickness in pregnancy, but delays in payment would lead, in 1973, to British supermarket chains mounting a boycott of the drinks produced by the group.

American Rock Death-Toll Rises

No fewer than four US rock musicians were reported dead this month - two in accidents and two from supposed drug abuse.

Miss Christine, singer with The GTOs (Girls Together Outrageously), died in Massachusetts of a heroin overdose on November 5, while the life of Crazy Horse guitarist Danny Whitten was claimed in similar fashion on November 18.

Though his group The New York Dolls were famed for excess, drummer Billy Murcia apparently departed on November 6 due to asphyxiation when a female companion tried to feed him coffee as he fell asleep.

Five days later, Berry Oakley - bass player with The Allman Brothers - died in a motor-cycle accident in Macon, Georgia, just three blocks from where the band's guitarist, Duane Allman, had perished in a similar accident, also aged 24, little more than 12 months previously.

NOVEMBER 3

Wedding Bells For James And Carly

Yet another of rock music's loving couples tied the knot today as singer-songwriters James Taylor and Carly Simon got married. Taylor, who was playing New York's legendary Radio City Music Hall that night, received a standing ovation when he announced the news.

Ironically, the new Mrs Taylor would hit the world-wide charts the following month with a song that hinted at the identity of another man she'd known very well. The self-penned *You're So Vain* was directed at Mick Jagger or was it Warren Beatty?

Perhaps in deference to her newly-acquired husband, Carly wasn't saying!

Last US Moon Mission Splashes Down

THE FINAL DRAMATIC EVENTS of the US' *Apollo* space programme were played out in the Pacific Ocean today when astronauts Cernan, Evans and Schmitt splashed down safely to end the 17th Apollo mission, and an exciting enterprise begun almost 11 years earlier by President John Kennedy.

Although NASA planned no further manned exploration of the surface of the Moon, the Apollo 17 astronauts left behind scientific metering equipment which they hoped would continue to feed back information to Earth on possible 'moonquakes', lunar gravity and cosmic rays.

One of the last Apollo astronauts, Harrison Schmitt, was primarily a scientist and was able to indulge his passion for geology during a total of 75 hours on the Moon's surface, in three separate trips from the orbiting command module.

In all, the multi-billion dollar programme inaugurated by President Kennedy in 1961 resulted in six manned voyages to the Moon.

Multi-Coloured Rock Opera Revived

Joseph And His Amazing Technicolor Dreamcoat, the rock opera that marked the first collaboration between Tim Rice and Andrew Lloyd Webber, was broadcast on British television today as a 45-minute production by the Young Vic company, featuring singer-actor Gary Bond as Joseph.

The musical, which retold the biblical story of Joseph and his coat of many colours, was being revived after the recent London West End success of Rice and Lloyd Webber's later work, *Jesus Christ Superstar.*

After becoming a staple of the British amateur dramatic society circuit repertoire in the 1980s, *Joseph* would again be revived as a major stage production in 1991, with Australian Jason Donovan taking the title role in London and seventies superstar Donny Osmond taking the bows in Toronto.

DECEMBER 29

Andes Crash Survivors Turn Cannibal

Survivors of a Uruguayan Air Force plane crash in the inhospitable Andes mountains turned to cannibalism as a last resort when their food ran out, it was learned today in Montevideo, capital of Uruguay.

Twenty-nine people died when the plane crashed on October 13, and the 16 survivors - half of whom were members of the Old Christians rugby team - were left with just the sweets and dried fruit which they had taken on the flight. But after two days those ran out and the soup which they concocted from lichen was not enough to sustain them in sub-zero temperatures.

Believing that they could not survive without protein, they were left with the grisly prospect of eating the bodies of those who had died in the crash. They survived for ten weeks on the remote mountainside before two members of the party finally risked a ten-day journey to raise the alarm. The story of their ordeal would be retold in the film *Alive*.

DECEMBER 24

Managua Devastated By Quake

As many as 10,000 people were reported killed today when a devastating earthquake hit Managua, the capital of the Central American country of Nicaragua, destroying up to three-quarters of its buildings.

For two and a half hours, the city was rocked by quakes which set off explosions and fires. Many fled to the countryside, but those who remained were to have their food supplies cut in an effort to get them to leave the now completely unsafe city.

Among the Westerners said to have been caught up in the devastation was reclusive industrialist billionaire Howard Hughes. He was one of an estimated 3,000 Americans reported safe, along with 100 British citizens in Managua when the quake hit.

DECEMBER 26

America Mourns Harry S Truman, Cold War Hero

ALL AMERICANS – whether Republican or Democrat – united in grief today as they learned of the death in a Kansas City hospital, Missouri, of former US President Harry S Truman. He was 88 years old and took with him a memory of a time when the US seemed to be the only nation capable of stemming the rising tide of Communism which threatened to engulf the world.

When Franklin D Roosevelt chose him as his running mate in the 1944 presidential election, Harry Truman (the middle 'S' meant nothing, but had been adopted for added 'weight') had come a long way since the days when, just back from World War I, he unsuccessfully attempted to start up a haberdashery business.

The loss of a potential haberdasher meant that the US, and the West, gained a statesman who, on the death of Roosevelt in 1945, was left with the responsibility of ending the war in the Far East and setting Europe on the road to recovery.

The war with Japan was abruptly concluded by the dropping of the two atomic bombs, the Marshall Plan devised by General George Marshall was put into operation to promote the rebuilding of Europe, and NATO was formed to protect the union of wartime alliances which had proved so successful. Re-elected as his own man in 1948, Truman faced down Stalin time and again, and led the US – and the United Nations – into the watershed of the Korean War.

Despite being eligible to run for another full term of office in 1952, Truman opted to retire, having served as President for seven stressful years during which he'd steered his nation masterfully through a period of world upheaval.

DECEMBER 30

America Ends North Vietnam Bomb Raids

After 12 days of the most devastating bombing of the Vietnam War, President Nixon called a halt to the raids on North Vietnam today. The decision to stop the air offensive may have been due to the extensive US losses suffered in bombing north of the 20th parallel - 15 B-52 bombers had been lost, plus 12 other aircraft, and 93 aircrew were reported dead, taken as POWs, or simply missing in action.

Military opinion was divided on the success of the raids, but international pressure had been mounting against the US. Even the Pope had criticized the delay in the successful conclusion of peace talks in Paris. That would appear to arrive in January 1973, though it would be a further two years before the North Vietnamese would emerge as victors.

DECEMBER 22

United Call For The Doc

After sacking manager Frank O'Farrell on December 19, top British soccer club Manchester United moved quickly to fill the gap today by appointing the outspoken and much-travelled Tommy Docherty as their third manager since the great Sir Matt Busby stepped down in 1969.

'Only one word can sum up my feelings – fantastic', exclaimed 'the Doc', who set out to boost his team with a trio of fellow Scots in Lou Macari, George Graham and Alex Forsyth. All cost six-figure fees, but Manchester United only just escaped relegation this season, and would subside to the Second Division the following year.

YOUR 1972 HOROSCOPE

Unlike most Western horoscope systems which group astrological signs into month-long periods based on the influence of 12 constellations, the Chinese believe that those born in the same year of their calendar share common qualities, traits and weaknesses with one of 12 animals - Rat, Ox, Tiger, Rabbit, Dragon, Snake, Horse, Sheep, Monkey, Rooster, Dog or Pig.

They also allocate the general attributes of five natural elements - Earth, Fire, Metal, Water, Wood - and an overall positive or negative aspect to each sign to summarize its qualities.

If you were born between January 27, 1971 and January 15, 1972, you are a Pig. As this book is devoted to the events of 1972, let's take a look at the sign which governs those born between January 16 that year and February 2, 1973 - The Year of the Rat:

THE RAT
JANUARY 16, 1972 - FEBRUARY 2, 1973
ELEMENT: METAL   ASPECT: (+)

Rats like to be pioneers, leaders of men and in the forefront of the action. As leaders they carry a somewhat majestic air, and they do well in any situation where they can be respected and admired. They are sociable, pleasant, amusing and born under the sign of charm.

Active, both physically and mentally, Rats tend to lead busy lives. They like a challenge, and to live dangerously, keeping their minds stimulated by having lots of projects always on the boil.

Rats are highly ambitious and are prepared to put a great deal of hard practical work into achieving their objectives - which they often do, being able to combine objectivity with imagination and perception. Sharply intuitive, Rats can see far ahead and go straight for their targets.

Best known for their charm, and possessors of a great sense of humour, Rats love to make an impact and leave a favourable impression. Home-loving and sensuous creatures, they can be extremely generous to the ones they love while being very frugal when it comes down to their basic living needs.

Rats are very loyal and renowned for standing by their loved ones. However, if they're confronted by real difficulties in life, they often find it hard to cope with the situation and become obsessive. Though considered tolerant and easygoing, there is always an implicit sense of anger and aggression which might break through.

Rat individuals generally control their feelings, presenting a cool front to the world even though they are very passionate. They find it hard to talk about their feelings, but do enjoy most forms of physical and sensual stimulation.

Rats are wiry and tenacious, and never give up easily. They are considered lucky, and their broad-minded approach to life makes them enjoy all kinds of new sensations and try to get as much out of life as they possibly can.

FAMOUS RATS

HM Queen Elizabeth, The Queen Mother
HRH The Prince of Wales
HRH Prince Harry
HRH The Duke of York
Marlon Brando
Oscar-winning actor, Native American Rights campaigner
Doris Day
actress, singer, dancer, businesswoman
Glenda Jackson
Oscar-winning actress, now socialist politician

Sir Andrew Lloyd Webber
composer, entrepreneur businessman
Gary Lineker
international soccer star, TV presenter
Wayne Sleep
modern dancer, choreographer, director
Yves St Laurent
fashion designer, businessman